# WE
# THEM
### and all of
# "US"

## Student Workbook
### Middle and High School Edition

Paperback ISBN  978-0-9727949-9-2

Printed in the United States of America.

*Cover Design: David Ter-Avanesyan*

For questions or additional information:
contact@bemontent.com

A product of

BEMONT

# CONTENTS

WORKSHEETS

PROJECTS

# WORKSHEETS

## Activity #1 through Activity #12

# Activity Worksheet #1

# Recognizing Concepts

## Why Are We Doing This?

The purpose of this exercise is to practice recognizing concepts such as "pluralism" and "assimilation" when these concepts are portrayed in real life.

## Activity

Read the statement below.

> STATEMENT:
>
> Some groups believe that if we could determine which minority characteristics are dysfunctional, we could develop ways of changing those characteristics. If minorities could change those characteristics, non-minority groups would be more understanding towards minorities and there would be less racism in society.

Now that you've read the statement, think of what you learned about pluralism and assimilation during class and answer the following question:

**Question:** Which of the concepts discussed in class (pluralism and assimilation) are represented in this statement? (Use the space below to write your answer.)

**Answer:** _____

# Notes

# Activity Worksheet #2

# The Challenge of Diversity

## Why Are We Doing This?

This activity will help you explore the challenges that can come along with trying to bring different groups together.

## Activity

Use the space below to list examples of conditions that can make it difficult for different groups to come together without having conflict. One column on the worksheet is for writing examples of inappropriate conditions you have seen or experienced. The other column is for writing possible solutions.

## From My Perspective

| Examples of environments and conditions that make it challenging for diverse groups to come together without having conflict | Possible Solutions |
| --- | --- |
|  |  |

# Notes

_____

_____

_____

_____

_____

_____

_____

_____

_____

_____

_____

_____

_____

_____

_____

_____

_____

_____

_____

# Activity Worksheet #3

# Beyond Our Borders

This activity will help you realize your ability to impact human well-being globally and understand the significance of becoming globally aware.

**Activity**

Identify a current event occurring outside of this country and briefly describe the current event you have selected.

## Current Event
Use this space to describe your current event.

**Question #1:** Although you live in a different country, in what ways are you affected by this event?

**Question #2:** In what ways can your thoughts, decisions, or talents impact individuals affected by this event?

# Notes

# Activity Worksheet #4

# Remembering History

## Why Are We Doing This?

This activity will help you understand the skills needed to achieve global awareness and realize the importance of our global community.

## Activity

Think back in history to find a time when people were not as globally mindful and could have benefitted from having greater global awareness.

---

### Historical Event
Use this space to describe your historical event.

---

**Question:** How could the outcomes of that event have been better/different if the people involved had practiced diversity?

---

**Diversity Definition:**

"Diversity" means more than just acknowledging or tolerating each other's differences. Diversity is a set of conscious practices that involve:

- mutual respect
- building alliances across differences
- being able to demonstrate compassion towards those who have qualities and conditions that are different from our own

# Notes

_____

_____

_____

_____

_____

_____

_____

_____

_____

_____

_____

_____

_____

_____

_____

_____

_____

_____

# Activity Worksheet #5

# Five Types of Theories About Racism and Other Social Biases

## Why Are We Doing This?

This activity will help you recognize theories and assumptions that cause racism and other social biases. Also, you will see how those theories impact the way we see and interact with others.

## Activity

There are many theories used to explain why racism and poor race relations continue to exist. We will explore five popular theories you may have heard or experienced. Fill in the blanks with the information that the instructor will provide.

### #1: Theories Based on _____ _____
**From these theories, you would conclude that minorities' failure to adapt is why they experience racism and discrimination.**

Assumptions:
Theories based on minority characteristics, therefore, assume that:

1. Majority group norms and behaviors are the _____ for judging minority group behavior and characteristics.

2. Behaviors that differ from majority group standards are viewed as _____ rather than as _____.

### #2: Theories Based on _____ _____
**From this perspective, the racism and discrimination someone may experience comes from the conscious and unconscious biases of individuals who have unfavorable beliefs and feelings about other groups based upon specific characteristics that differ from their own.**

Assumptions:
Theories addressing individual bias, therefore, assume that:

1. The individual who practices discrimination does not represent the _____ _____ but is seen as different from the norm.

2. Although many individuals may experience racism and other forms of discrimination, these practices are not viewed as part of most _____ _____.

## #3: Theories Based on _____ _____

From these theories, physical separation and a lack of social contact between different groups is what causes misconceptions about one another and a willingness to believe theories and rumors that validate those misconceptions.

<u>Assumptions:</u>
Theories addressing social isolation, therefore assume that:

1. A community represents a social group more than a _____ _____.

2. Physical separation makes it harder for individuals in one group to understand and recognize the _____ of individuals in a _____ _____.

## #4: Theories Based on _____ _____

From this perspective, institutions implement policies and procedures that exclude or limit minority group participation and opportunities to succeed.

<u>Assumptions:</u>
Theories addressing institutional practices, therefore, assume that:

1. Racism and other forms of bias have become _____ into the everyday operations of our institutions.

## # 5: Theories Based on _____ _____

These types of theories conclude that discrimination comes from the threatening feelings that develop when groups compete in an environment where there are limited resources.

<u>Assumptions:</u>
Theories addressing group competition, therefore assume that:

1. Groups respond negatively to one another when they are trying to protect their _____ _____ _____.

2. Other groups are your _____.

# Why These Theories Matter

As the next generation of leaders, you must recognize your ability to influence policies and practices in your neighborhood, town, country, and around the world. Your level of awareness affects your ability to contribute in ways that are meaningful to the people your decisions will impact.

# Notes

_____

_____

_____

_____

_____

_____

_____

_____

_____

_____

_____

_____

_____

_____

_____

_____

_____

_____

# Notes

_____

_____

_____

_____

_____

_____

_____

_____

_____

_____

_____

_____

_____

_____

_____

_____

_____

_____

# Activity Worksheet #6

# Recognizing Theories in Action

## Why Are We Doing This?

Sorry! I can't tell you now, but I promise to tell you after this activity.

## Activity

STATEMENT:

Within the literature on race relations, some authors have mentioned that historically Latinx/Hispanics have been excluded from books discussing racism. Some authors conclude there has been a lack of awareness regarding the Latinx/Hispanic experience of discrimination.

Based on the perspective mentioned in the statement above, answer the following question:

**Question:** Regardless of whether you agree or disagree with the authors' perspective, can you think of reasons why there might have been a lack of awareness regarding the Latinx/Hispanic experience of discrimination? *Write your response in the space provided below:*

# Notes

_____

_____

_____

_____

_____

_____

_____

_____

_____

_____

_____

_____

_____

_____

# Activity Worksheet #7

# Experiencing Difference

## Why Are We Doing This?

This activity will help you get in touch with many of the feelings associated with being identified as "different."

## Activity

Think of a time in your life when you felt "different" from the people around you. Use the space below to describe that experience. (How old were you? Where were you? Who or what made you feel different?)

How did that experience make you feel? (List three words that best describe how you felt when that experience happened.)

1 _____

2 _____

3 _____

# Notes

# Activity Worksheet #8

# The Look of Diversity

Using the grid below, identify two types of "differences" you would like to address (gender, ethnicity, special needs, etc.). Use Columns #2 through #5 to provide examples of how it looks when we are truly practicing the principles of "diversity." You may use the two categories provided in Column #1 (ethnicity and physical abilities/disabilities) or select two of your own by writing in the empty cells in Column #1.

| #1 Type of Difference | #2 Understanding Difference | #3 Appreciating Difference | #4 Practicing mutual respect | #5 Building alliances across differences |
|---|---|---|---|---|
| Ethnicity | | | | |
| Physical Abilities/ Disabilities | | | | |
| | | | | |
| | | | | |

# Notes

_____

_____

_____

_____

_____

_____

_____

_____

_____

_____

_____

_____

_____

_____

_____

_____

# Activity Worksheet #9A

# Creating Social Categories
# East vs. West

## Why Are We Doing This?

This activity will help you understand how social categories are created.

## Activity

Name one city on the east coast of the United States: _____

Name one city on the west coast of the United States: _____

Make a list of the ways people from the east coast city listed above differ from those in the west coast city listed above.

East _____

West _____

East _____

West _____

East _____

West _____

East _____

West _____

East _____

West _____

# Notes

_____

_____

_____

_____

_____

_____

_____

_____

_____

_____

_____

_____

_____

_____

_____

_____

_____

# Activity Worksheet #9B

# Creating Social Categories
# Urban vs. Rural

## Why Are We Doing This?

This activity will help you understand how social categories are created.

## Activity

Name one urban city in the United States: _____

Name one rural town in the United States: _____

Make a list of the ways that people from the urban city listed above differ from those in the rural town listed above.

Urban _____

Rural _____

Urban _____

Rural _____

Urban _____

Rural _____

Urban _____

Rural _____

Urban _____

Rural _____

# Notes

# Activity Worksheet #10

# Acting Out the Stereotypes

## Why Are We Doing This?

This activity will help you understand the effects of stereotyping.

## Activity

Identify an interaction you have seen, among youth or adults, that you feel is an example of stereotyping or the consequences of stereotyping.

Now, using the space provided below, briefly describe the interaction.

Here are some questions you may want to consider. Use a separate sheet of paper for your answers.

**Question #1:** Based on what you learned in class about stereotyping and social categories, what effects of social categories or stereotyping are occurring in this interaction?

**Question #2:** In what ways do the concepts and experiences within this interaction apply to conflicts that may occur on campus or in your community?

# Notes

# Activity Worksheet #11

# Examining Cross-Cultural Communications

This activity will help you better recognize the verbal and non-verbal behaviors we sometimes use to communicate with individuals who speak a different language.

## Activity

What kinds of <u>verbal</u> behavior do you use to communicate with someone who speaks a different language? (Example: talking loudly)

What kinds of <u>non-verbal</u> behavior do you use to communicate with someone who speaks a different language? (Example: using hand gestures)

# Notes

_____

_____

_____

_____

_____

_____

_____

_____

_____

_____

_____

_____

_____

_____

_____

_____

_____

_____

# Activity Worksheet #12

# Experiencing Language as a Barrier

## STUDENT READINGS

### Reading #1:
### LANGUAGE AND NONVERBAL BEHAVIOR

We frequently overlook the power of nonverbal behavior (facial expressions, the amount of physical space during conversations, etc.). Many of us believe that communication primarily occurs through verbal messages. However, it is nonverbal behavior that helps us interpret the verbal message. This is best demonstrated when statements are meant to be sarcastic or said jokingly. For example, if I tell you, "I like your hair," how do you determine whether you should take the statement as a compliment or as a display of sarcasm? Some of the cues you will most likely use to make this determination will be nonverbal. You may look at facial expressions or listen to changes in voice tone.

Let's consider that every culture has its method of sending nonverbal cues. The same nonverbal behavior that communicates sarcasm in one culture may communicate admiration or respect in another culture. Given these differences, you can see there is tremendous potential for nonverbal behavior to play a significant role in misunderstandings between cultures.

### Reading #2:
### LANGUAGE AND NONVERBAL BEHAVIOR

Discussions regarding the nature of misunderstandings between cultures seldom include an analysis of the role that paralanguage (the tone, pitch, speed, volume, facial expressions, and gestures used in speaking) may play. For English-speaking Americans, a drop in the pitch of their voice and how quickly the pitch drops can affect how we interpret the meaning of their statement. The faster the pitch drops at the end of a sentence, the more likely someone is to feel that you are frustrated or angry. The slower the pitch drops, the more likely someone is to interpret the statement as being pleasant.

Different cultures use paralanguage in different ways. For example, to an English-speaking American, other cultures may appear to speak harshly to one another due to the difference in where they drop or hold their pitch. When other cultures speak English, they frequently maintain the style of paralanguage used when speaking their native language, although the words are English. If we are unaware of how different tones, pitches, speeds, and volumes are used among other cultures, we will expect all English speakers from other countries to use the same style of paralanguage that is familiar to English-speaking Americans. Given these differences, you can see there is tremendous potential for paralanguage to play a significant role in misunderstandings between cultures.

# Notes

_____

_____

_____

_____

_____

_____

_____

_____

_____

_____

_____

_____

_____

_____

_____

_____

_____

# PROJECT #1

## Creative Cultural Expressions

# Project #1

## Student Handout
## Creative Cultural Expressions
## Project Description Sheet

Topic: _____

_____

Materials Needed: _____

_____

_____

_____

Participants: _____    _____

_____    _____

_____    _____

_____    _____

Project Description (use the space below):

# PROJECT #2

## Student Diversity and Anti-Bias Report

**SAMPLE** - **Cover Sheet: Form #1**

# A REPORT ABOUT
# DIVERSITY AND ANTI-BIAS AT

(School Name):_____

### THE STUDENT PERSPECTIVE

Course Title: _____

Date: _____

Instructor: _____

# SAMPLE – Introduction: Form #2

## Introduction

The purpose of this report was not to criticize, but to provide students with an opportunity to openly and constructively discuss issues that may assist in causing or continuing tensions on campus. The contents of this document are not for the purpose of establishing right and wrong. The reader may even disagree with the perceptions of this class. Hopefully, regardless of one's agreements or disagreements, this report will be viewed as valued data providing insight into the thinking of this group of (school name):_____ students.

       This report represents a collective effort by the (year):_____(course title):_____ class to become active participants in helping to create and sustain a positive social and learning environment on our campus.

# SAMPLE - Background of the Report: Form #3

## Background of the Report

This section is intended to provide the reader with an understanding of the procedures used to develop this report and the characteristics of the participants. This section is divided into three categories: 1) Class Demographics, 2) Discussion Question, and 3) Procedures.

## Class Demographics

The class consisted of (# of students)_____ participants. Table 1 outlines the demographic composition of those students. There were (#)_____ juniors, (#)_____ seniors, (#)_____ sophomores, (#)_____ freshmen, (#)_____ eighth graders, (#)_____seventh graders, and (#)_____six graders. There were_____% more (gender)_____ than (gender)_____ with _____% choosing not to identify their gender. (Ethnic group)_____ comprised the largest percentage of the class (_____%) although a range of ethnic groups were represented. Other ethnic groups and their percentages include: _____ (_____%), _____ (_____%), _____ (_____%), and _____ (_____%).

## Discussion Question

The major question that established the primary focus of this report was: "What are the diversity and anti-bias issues and concerns which need to be addressed at (school name):_____."

## Procedures

Responses to the major question resulted in a list of comments, issues, questions, and solutions. The issues were separated by topic; the comments and solutions were matched with the issues they appeared to address; and the questions were compiled into a list to be included at the end of the report.

The class was then divided into small groups, ranging from five to eight members, to discuss the issues and solutions using the following list of questions as a guideline:

1)  Is the issue relevant enough to be included in the report?
2)  Are the suggested solutions appropriate and relevant?
3)  Are there other solutions that can be offered?
4)  Are there any additional comments we would like to make regarding the issue?

After the small group discussions, the class agreed on the various issues and solutions we felt should be included in this report.

Diversity and Anti-Bias Report: Worksheet 3A

Table 1: Frequencies and Percentages of Class Demographics     (Total Class Size: _____)

| VARIABLE | FREQUENCY | PERCENTAGE |
|---|---|---|
| **Ethnicity** | | |
| Latinx/Hispanic | _____ | _____ |
| European American | _____ | _____ |
| African American | _____ | _____ |
| Asian/Pacific Islander | _____ | _____ |
| Native American/Alaskan Native | _____ | _____ |
| Other | _____ | _____ |
| **Gender** | | |
| Female | _____ | _____ |
| Male | _____ | _____ |
| Prefer not to respond | _____ | _____ |
| **Gender Identity** | | |
| Woman | _____ | _____ |
| Man | _____ | _____ |
| Transgender | _____ | _____ |
| Non-binary/non-conforming | _____ | _____ |
| Prefer not to respond | _____ | _____ |
| **Grade** | | |
| Senior | _____ | _____ |
| Junior | _____ | _____ |
| Sophomore | _____ | _____ |
| Freshmen | _____ | _____ |
| Eighth Grade | _____ | _____ |
| Seventh Grade | _____ | _____ |
| Sixth Grade | _____ | _____ |

Diversity and Anti-Bias Report: Worksheet 3B

Chart 1: Chart Plotting the Target Areas of Student Concerns

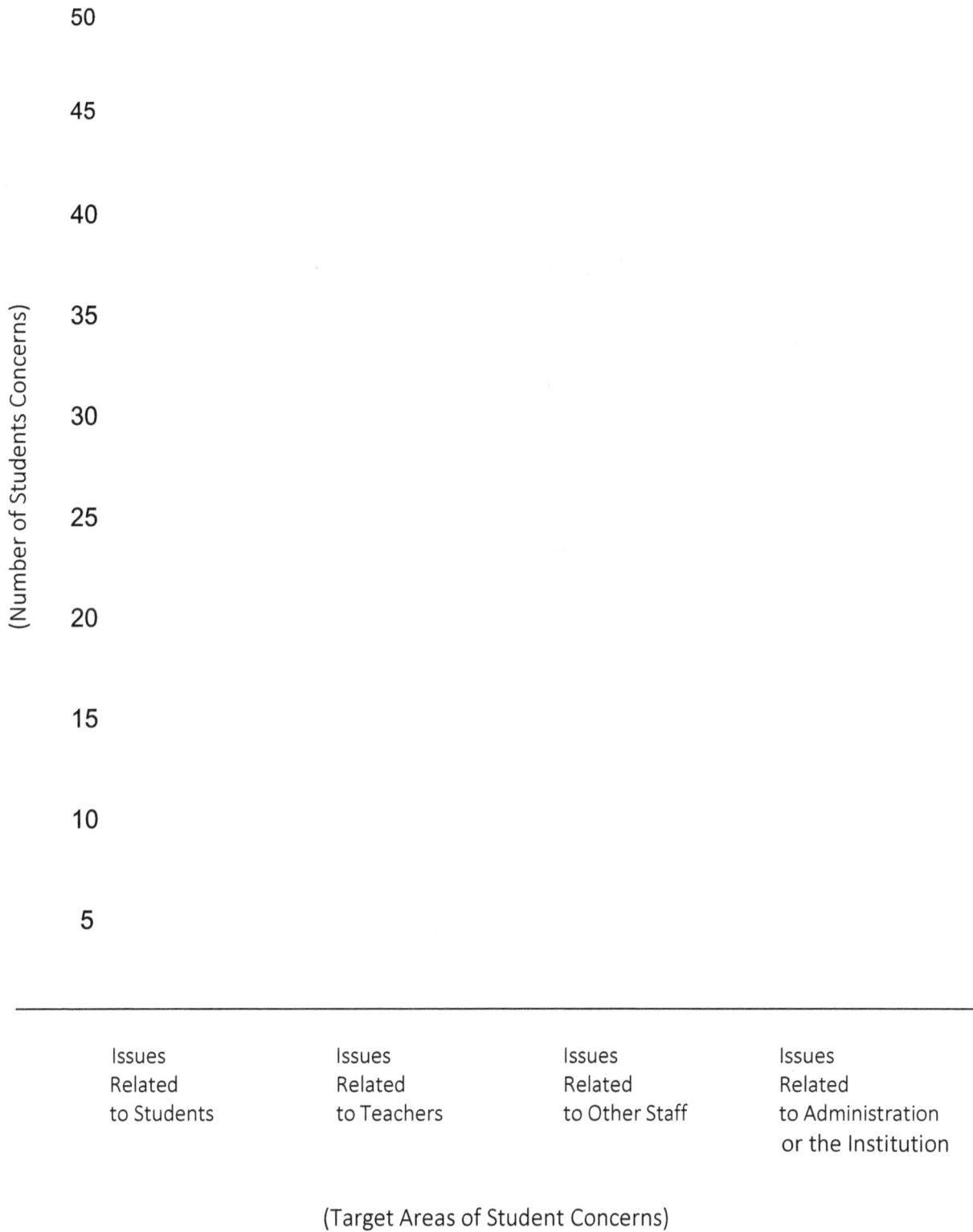

50

45

40

35

30

(Number of Students Concerns)

25

20

15

10

5

_____

| Issues | Issues | Issues | Issues |
| Related | Related | Related | Related |
| to Students | to Teachers | to Other Staff | to Administration |
| | | | or the Institution |

(Target Areas of Student Concerns)

# SAMPLE – Format for the body of the report: Form #4

## Report

ISSUE #1: A general lack of cultural awareness at Boulevard High School

### COMMENT

I feel there is a lack of awareness of the wants and needs of other groups on the Boulevard High School campus. This becomes particularly clear when many students say they do not know why a particular ethnic group is upset about something.

### RECOMMENDATION

More opportunities to discuss topics that help raise awareness around diversity issues on campus.

ISSUE #2: Special needs students being bullied at Boulevard High School

### COMMENT

There is a lack of sensitivity regarding the experience of special needs students on our campus.

### RECOMMENDATIONS

The school needs to implement a stronger anti-bullying campaign.

We should implement a buddy system where typical kids are encouraged to look out for their special needs peers and anonymously report any inappropriate interactions.

A product of

bemontent.com

If you have a story or a thought to share
as a result of using this workbook
we would love to hear from you!


contact@bemontent.com

www.ingramcontent.com/pod-product-compliance
Lightning Source LLC
Chambersburg PA
CBHW080927050426
42334CB00055B/2832